JUV/E Hanson, Joan.
PE
1216   Plurals
.H3
1979

Cop.1

3.95

DATE			

CHICAGO PUBLIC LIBRARY
HILD REGIONAL BRANCH
4544 LINCOLN AVE.
CHICAGO, ILLINOIS 60625

© THE BAKER & TAYLOR CO.

mouse...mice, leaf...leaves, and other

WORDS THAT CHANGE IN NUMBER

PLURALS

Joan Hanson

Published by
Lerner Publications Company
Minneapolis, Minnesota

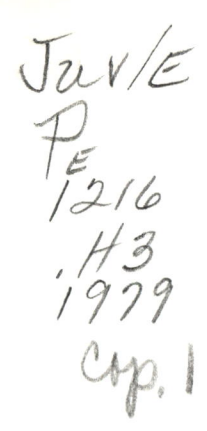

*For Timmy
and his Magic B*

Copyright © 1979 by Lerner Publications Company

All rights reserved. International copyright secured. Manufactured in the United States of America. Published simultaneously in Canada by J. M. Dent & Sons (Canada) Ltd., Don Mills, Ontario.

International Standard Book Number: 0-8225-1114-2
Library of Congress Catalog Card Number: 78-70463

Plurals are words that indicate a change in number, usually from one to more than one. As the examples *tooth...teeth* and *child...children* show, words change from the singular form to the plural form in different ways. The most common change is to simply add an *s*, as in the example *pig...pigs*.

Tooth

Teeth

Pig

Pigs

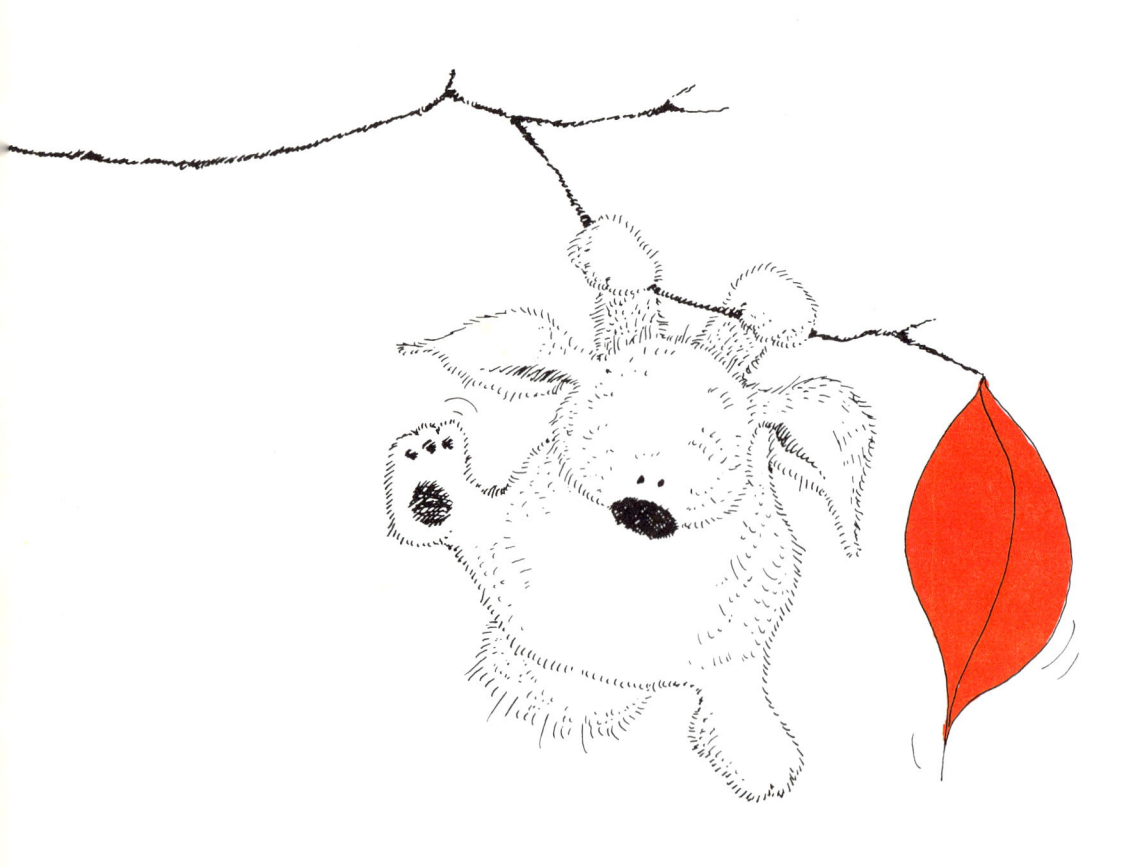

Leaf

Leaves

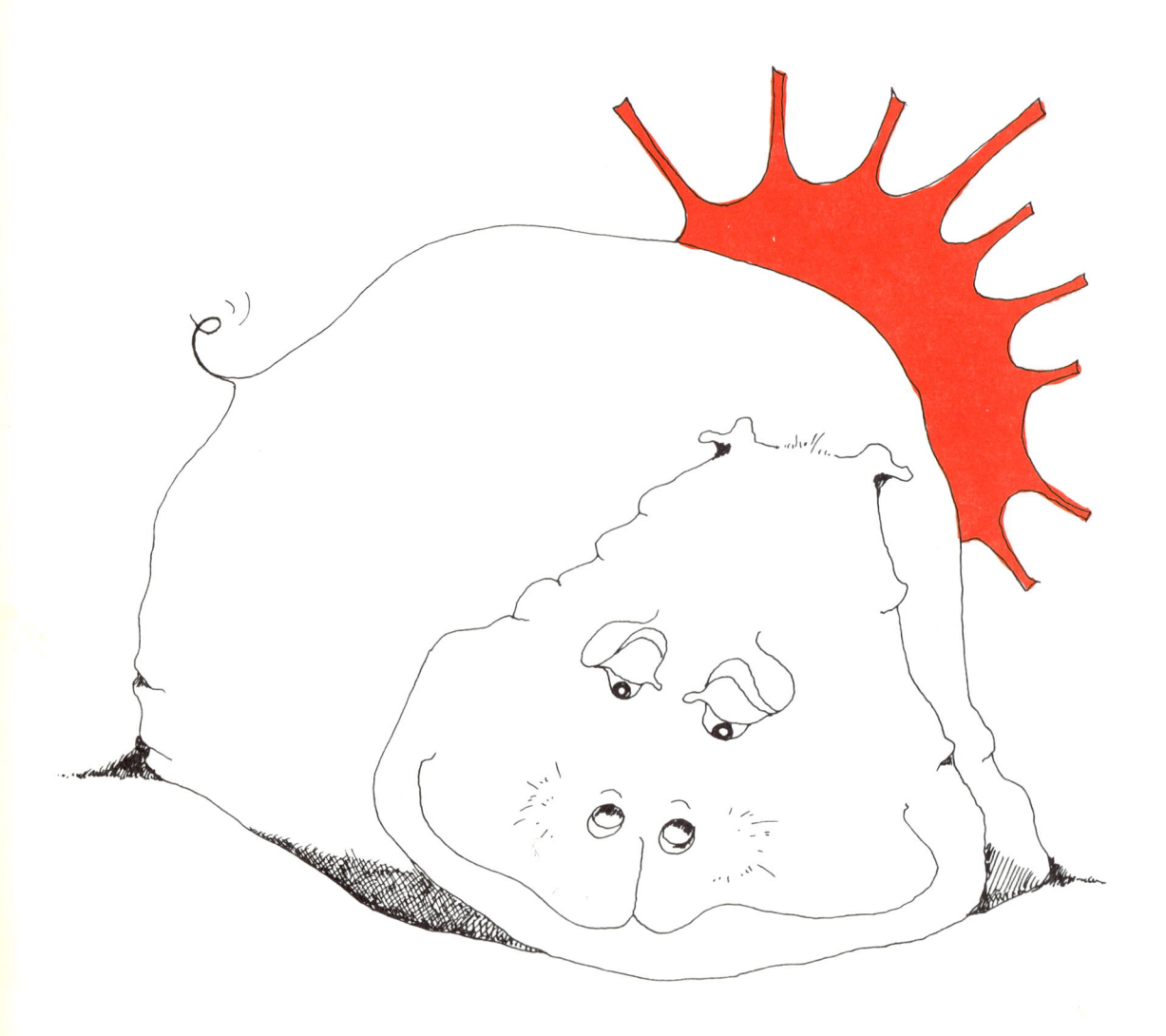

Hippo

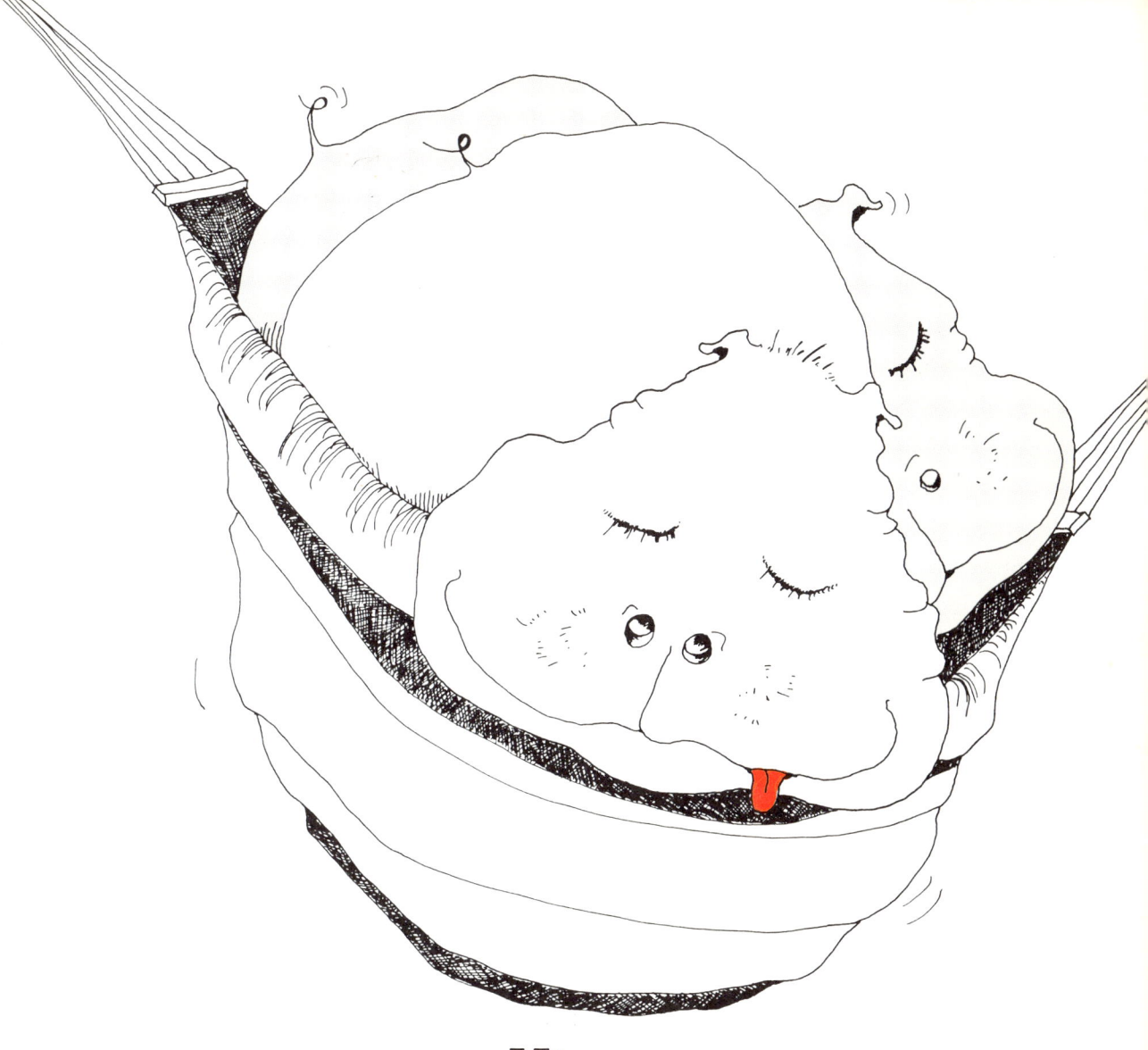

Hippos

Witch

Witches

Glasses

Glasses

Foot

Feet

Chief

Chiefs

Mouse

Mice

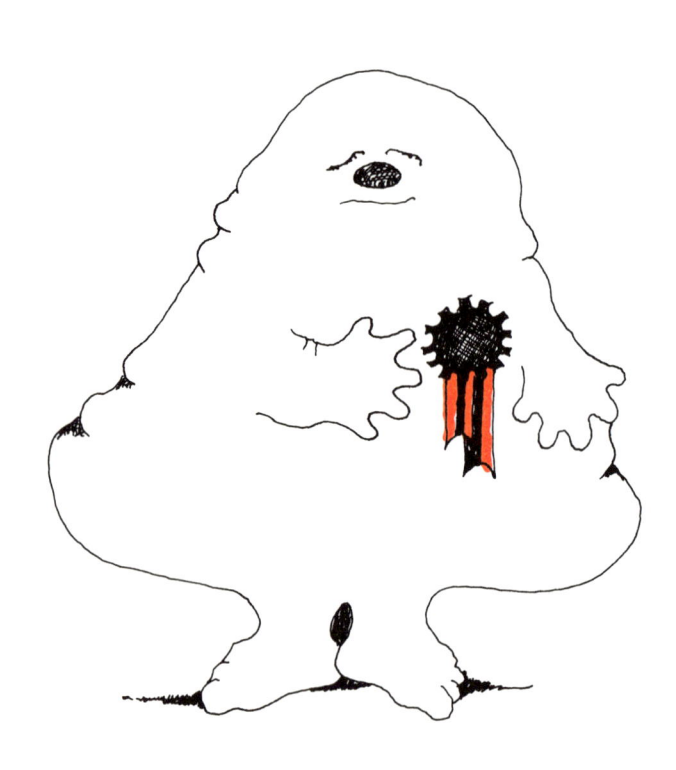

Hero

Heroes

Baby

Babies

Key

Keys

Child

Children

BOOKS IN THIS SERIES

ANTONYMS
hot and cold and other
WORDS THAT ARE DIFFERENT
as night and day

MORE ANTONYMS
wild and tame and other
WORDS THAT ARE AS DIFFERENT IN MEANING
as work and play

STILL MORE ANTONYMS
together and apart and other
WORDS THAT ARE AS DIFFERENT IN MEANING
as rise and fall

HOMONYMS
hair and hare and other
WORDS THAT SOUND THE SAME
but look as different as bear and bare

MORE HOMONYMS
steak and stake and other
WORDS THAT SOUND THE SAME
but look as different as chili and chilly

STILL MORE HOMONYMS
night and knight and other
WORDS THAT SOUND THE SAME
but look as different as ball and bawl

HOMOGRAPHS
bow and bow and other
WORDS THAT LOOK THE SAME
but sound as different as sow and sow

HOMOGRAPHIC HOMOPHONES
fly and fly and other
WORDS THAT LOOK AND SOUND THE SAME
but are as different in meaning as bat and bat

British-American SYNONYMS
french fries and chips and other
WORDS THAT MEAN THE SAME THING
but look and sound
as different as truck and lorry

MORE SYNONYMS
shout and yell and other
WORDS THAT MEAN THE SAME THING
but look and sound
as different as loud and noisy

SIMILES
as gentle as a lamb, spin like a top, and other
"LIKE" OR "AS" COMPARISONS
between unlike things

MORE SIMILES
roar like a lion, as loud as thunder, and other
"LIKE" OR "AS" COMPARISONS
between unlike things

SOUND WORDS
jingle, buzz, sizzle, and other
WORDS THAT IMITATE THE SOUNDS AROUND US

MORE SOUND WORDS
munch, clack, thump, and other
WORDS THAT IMITATE THE SOUNDS AROUND US

PLURALS
mouse...mice, leaf...leaves, and other
WORDS THAT CHANGE IN NUMBER

POSSESSIVES
monkey's banana...monkeys' bananas,
thief's mask...thieves' masks, and other
WORDS THAT SHOW OWNERSHIP

Lerner Publications Company
241 First Avenue North, Minneapolis, Minnesota 55401